Augusta Cordelia Davis

Poems from Yare

Augusta Cordelia Davis

Poems from Yare

ISBN/EAN: 9783744710954

Printed in Europe, USA, Canada, Australia, Japan

Cover: Foto ©Thomas Meinert / pixelio.de

More available books at **www.hansebooks.com**

POEMS FROM YARE,

BY

ALICE CHADBOURNE.
(AUGUSTA C. DAVIS.)

PORTLAND:
FORD & RICH, PUBLISHERS.
1890.

To the memory of
MY SISTER,
WHOSE LIFE WAS A SWEETER AND TRUER POEM
THAN ANY I CAN EVER HOPE TO WRITE,
I Dedicate
THIS LITTLE VOLUME.

The following poems written at intervals and without thought of publication in permanent form, have been collected into the present volume, at the suggestion of friends, whose kindness, perhaps, has accorded them a merit far greater than they have any right to claim.

Deprived of sight, I cannot well give them the revision, that might render them more worthy of the critical reader; yet, as expressions of earnest feeling and of real experience, I cannot help hoping they may carry a cheery message, or word of comfort to some sorrowful soul, who is waiting, alone, in the shadow.

ALICE CHADBOURNE.

VIOLETS.

COME, sisters, come! there ne'er was born a
    morning
  So purely bright as this;
I long to watch the rosy glory dawning
  Under the sun's warm kiss.

I know a hiding-place of fragrant treasures,
  The spring's late, lovely flowers;
Oh, come! the season brims with dainty pleasures
  For happy hearts like ours.

I watched them go, while bitter thoughts were
    springing,
  I, too, loved all things fair:
Yearned for the sweetness flowers abroad were
    flinging
  On the delicious air.

Why must the sunshine pure and bright and
    glowing
  That touched them but to bless
And fill each heart with gladness overflowing,
  Bring me so sharp distress?

Why must such wealth of pleasant things be
    yielded?
No woodland flowers for me.
Ah, faithless heart, by the cool grasses shielded,
    What sight sprang fair to see?

Beyond my window, 'neath the clustered whiteness
    Of fragrant cherry-trees,
Blooming in beauty, 'mid the shaded brightness
    Kissed by the charméd breeze;

Lifting their fair heads to receive the blessing
    God sends and ne'er forgets;
Giving back incense for the sun's caressing,
    Nestled sweet violets.

Shamed and yet thrilled with gladness at the
    vision.
The tears came springing fast,
Quick footsteps brought me to the spot Elysian,
    All bitter murmurs past.

For me, for me, O blue eyes deep and tender!
    For me, O rare perfume;
Ah, if, like you, I, too, sweet praise might render
    For all this gift of bloom.

God does remember; in our sorest trial
    Peace comes, or late, or soon;
His loving hand, 'mid life's most stern denial,
    Bestows some blessed boon.

AGNES.

As I sit in my chamber at night,
    While the stars softly bloom in the sky,
And the moon, with pale glory alight,
        Hangs, trembling, in blue depths on high,
        I list, as I've listened before,
        For a gay little knock at my door
And the sweet, happy ringing of Agnes' voice
            singing
        A song which will sound nevermore.

Oh, it must be a terrible dream!
        Those long weeks of anguish and dread ;
When we watched, with hope's flickering gleam,
        Till they spoke the strange words, "She
            is dead."
        But the musical voice was so clear,
        And the glad little tones were so dear,
That, while I am waiting, my very breath bating,
        They seem to be echoing near.

And, I answer "Come in pretty bird!
        With your odd, little fanciful lay;
It is time the sweet carol I heard,—
        Come, sing me your song of to-day:"
Then quickly the door flashes wide,
And swiftly there springs to my side,
A wee, dainty maiden, with happy thoughts laden
        And life flowing full like the tide.

"Oh! I am so glad it is night,
        And I can come straight to your room,"
She begins, in a tone of delight,
        That rings through the silvery gloom;
As I fold close the delicate form,
        'Mid a shower of soft kisses warm,
With loving arms twining, and wondrous eyes
        shining,
        As bright as the stars after storm.

Then she gives her strange fancy full play,
        And sings me a song of the sea;
A rhymeless, but musical lay,
        As perfect as perfect can be;
And there comes o'er the sweet, thoughtful face
        A tender and exquisite grace,
As of one who, in dreaming, sees soft splendor
        streaming
        From out of some glorified place.

Ah! the quaint little songs are all sung;
　　Closed to us are the beautiful eyes;
But the clear voice is chanting among
　　Christ's little ones called to the skies;
　And though our hearts ache and we miss
　The joy and the song and the kiss,
Yet sweet is the feeling that God is revealing
　　His love, in sore trials like this.

THE BLESSING OF THE ICE CREAM.

ONE summer day, into a thronged saloon,
    A lovely mother with her children came;
Two little fairies, blithe as birds in June,
    And fair as fairest flower that I could name.

Before the eager little ones was placed
    The frosty dainty, sought by young and old,
When Winter yields the glitt'ring throne he graced,
    And languid airs our drooping forms enfold.

A moment's pause, and, then, a strange command
    Rang softly out.   The youngest baby said,
Laying her tiny snow-flake of a hand
    Upon her sister's, "Bessie, bow your head!"

And there, amid the merry, careless crowd,
    The children's golden heads were lowly
        bent;
While they besought, sweet-voiced and quiet
        browed,
    A blessing on the feast their Father sent.

A hush fell on the stirred and list'ning throng;
    Laughter and jest were ended, and a tear
Stole down unchecked, from eyes unmoistened
      long
    By holy mem'ries.   Out into the clear,

Hot noontide, through the surge and whirl
    Of busy life, was borne in many a heart
A tender picture of that baby-girl
    Yielding her tribute in the city mart.

EDITH.

U P from the fairy realm of childhood,
  Into the glowing land of youth;
As sweet as a rose from the dewy wildwood,
   She comes with her treasure of love and
    truth.

Where has she garnered such store of gladness
   In a world that is heavy with care like ours?
Is it her mission to charm the sadness
   From aching hearts and to scatter flowers

Where, bare and lonely, the pathway leads us
   Through dreary regions of loss and pain
And bring, with a comforting page she reads us,
   The light to the darkened day again?

So it seems to me, as I wait her coming,
   At autumn twilight, or summer noon;
As blithe as the bees in their rythmic humming,
   She keeps our natures in perfect tune.

With joyous grace and with ready measure,
   She joins the dance in the festive hall;
Ever a star in the world of pleasure,
   Ever a welcome guest to all.

Then she turns again to her loving labor,
　　When merry music and dance are done
And she comes and sits with her prosy neighbor,
　　As if nothing were better beneath the sun,

And to cheer the lot of the heavy laden,
　　To lift the burden, to gild the gloom,
Were the wonted tasks of a care-free maiden,
　　A graceful girl in her early bloom.

O heart unselfish and blue eyes tender!
　　O sunny spirit and helpful hand!
May the gracious care of our God defend her
　　　From all that could harm her on sea or
　　　　land.

From every ill that would mar her being,
　　Or check the growth of her noble powers;
From joy, that would lessen her soul's clear-see-
　　　ing,
　　Or barter its wealth for a wreath of flowers.

May every good that can speed her faring
　　To lofty levels and prospect wide,
Be hers, 'till the crown for the christian's wearing
　　Shall brighten her brow on the other side.

LED HOME.

W̶HEN I recall the young life passed away,
  There comes to me a picture dim and
   sweet;
The lovely closing of a summer's day,
  And a lithe form across the shadowy
   street.

A lovely twilight, but obscure and blind
  The path unto my darkened eyes appeared;
In vain I sought an entrance safe to find,
  My home receded as its rest I neared.

Soft, on the silence, stole a sudden sound,
  And a low voice rang like a silver bell:—
"Oh! stay a moment, please; the way you've found
  Leads into danger;" then the darkness
   fell.

But close beside me spoke my helpful friend:—
  "I have been watching you, afraid of
   harm;"
And thus my anxious quest found happy end;
  Thanks to the little guiding hand and arm.

To-day, while tears fall fast at thought of her,
  The tender mother; the devoted wife;
Sweet words of comfort 'mid the shadows stir;
  And clear the problem of this broken life.

There is a Friend, who watches all our ways,
  And, though the path we tread seem safe
   and fair;
He sees our danger and our progress stays,
  Leading us home with gracious love and
   care.

A MEMORY.

IN the fair month of roses, long ago,
  Amid the song and sunshine and the glow
Of summer tints, there came a little child
Into my home, sweet as the violet wild.
     No bird upon its tree,
E'er found life half so rare a boon as she.

My pen has little power to paint the grace
Of this wee maiden, or the changeful face
That flashed a joyous greeting to the sun,
Yet grew so strangely glad when day was done;
     And, in the star-lit night,
Mirrored the shy, sweet thoughts that shunned
     the light.

In her brief life before, she had not known
The freedom of a home she called her own;
And reveled in it, now, as city child
Drinks in the freshness of the country wild ;
     We watched her blithesome play,
And held our treasure closer, day by day.

There was a window in our cottage roof,
Where Agnes loved to weave the warp and woof
Of her quaint fancies; and the iron bar,
Holding the casement when it swung afar,
  Stirred me to vague alarm,
Lest it might work our little poet harm.

The mother called her lovely child to stand
Beneath the window, and, with careful hand,
Measured the space above the sunny head;
And then she turned to me and, smiling, said,
  "Do not be troubled, dear!
She will not reach that height within the year."

Too soon the lavish summer spent its gold;
I had not thought one little heart could hold
Such wealth of joy as dowered our little maid,
Whether she sang in sunshine or in shade;
  All fairest things above
Seemed to bend over her in silent love.

And when the regal season breathed farewell,
Though warm and sweet still lay her rosy spell,
The watchful Father, loving more than we,
Called to His little one, "Come unto Me!"
  My boding fears were vain.
No harm can reach her, now; no sin can stain.

MY DREAM.

How vivid was my dream!
    You came, I thought, from fresh and fra-
        grant fields;
From the low music of Yare's pleasant stream,
Where the wee violet its incense yields,
    And throws its purple gleam.

I heard your gentle tread,
Just as I heard it on still afternoons,
When life and hope were to each other wed,
In cool Septembers and in glowing Junes,
    Before earth's sunshine fled.

I heard your little feet,
And all my heart grew light and glad once more.
I could not linger, but, with footsteps fleet,
I sprang to clasp you at the open door;
    Joy's benison was sweet!

There, in the sunset warm,
With the old, winsome grace, I saw you stand;
The golden glory wrapped your slender form,
And, on my soul, at touch of your dear hand,
    Fell calm, as after storm.

I saw the happy play,
Of light and love in your dark, lustrous eyes;
I heard your clear voice, blithe as morning, say,
In tender little accents of surprise,
    "Have I been long away?"

Dearest, is it *not* long?
O sweetest spirit that e'er blest my days;
O gentlest soul that ever hated wrong;
O sunny heart that gladdened all our ways,
    Sister! is it not long?

Is it not long to miss
The tenderness that crowned me day by day;
The light of loving eyes, the clasp, the kiss,
The interchange of thought and fancy's play?
    Yet, not for Heaven's own bliss

Would I inure, again,
My treasured one to earth's unending care;
Far better life-long loneliness and pain,
Than shadow fall on lot so sweet and fair,
    Or loss defraud her gain.

RESPICIENS.

THE rosy firelight shadows soft are gleaming
  Upon the half-shut door,
The clear white moonlight, through the window
   streaming,
  Lies all along the floor.

Do not bring lamps. 'Tis sweet to bathe in bright-
   ness
  So pure and yet so warm.
Let fancy give the heart its early lightness;
  Forget life's cold and storm.

How many nights, in just such cloudless glory,
  We sat together here
And wrote the sweetest part of all life's story,
  With pens sun-tipt and clear!

How many times, with fervent speech and golden,
  One came at set of sun.
How many times, from "language quaint and olden,"
  Read what the world has done!

How many times, when pleasant talk was ending,
    And books, a priceless throng,
Lay with closed lids, our thoughts and feelings
    blending,
    Soft blossomed into song!

My friend. Your more than friend. What wealth
    of treasure
    God gave us in those days!
Shall we forget, 'mid sorrow's bitter measure,   ·
    To render grateful praise?

What, if a few, brief years held all our gladness,
    And then long anguish came?
The full, rich strain breathed not one note of sad-
    ness,
    But brimmed with sweet acclaim.

Is it not better to have known and cherished
    One rare and noble heart,
Though from our side the earthly form has perished,
    And we must walk apart,

Than to have had, through all earth's weary changes,
    Those meaner friendships given,
That could not lead us up to higher ranges,
    Nor help us on to Heaven?

Ah, brave, strong heart! Ah, brain with rich thought
glowing!
Shot through by traitor-hand!
God took the costly gift of His bestowing,
Offered for father-land.

He comes no more, his warm, bright presence lend-
ing
New grace, as joys unfold;
He comes no more, for us so freely spending
His intellect's fine gold.

Silence and cold, where smile, and glow, and bless-
ing
Answered your lightest speech;
Where glance and touch were but the mute caressing,
Such love alone can teach.

The dainty little child, white-robed and gifted
With all the mother's grace,
May never to her father's heart be lifted,
Or cheer his noble face.

But when, at length, the long, long path is ended,
The joy, earth but begun,
To fairer climes and blessed hearts ascended,
Shall brighten as the sun.

GRACE.

"I am so very little, auntie, dear!
　　How can a child, as young as I, and small,
Do any good, or help to aid and cheer
　　The people, who are wise and strong and tall?"

"Ah, tiny Mabel! with your earnest face
　　And lifted gaze, you mind me well, of one,
Who seemed to me—dear, little blue-eyed Grace—
　　The sweetest comforter beneath the sun.

"As young as you, and very fair to see;
　　Strangers, in passing, paused, and paused again,
Charmed by the smiling glance and motion free,
　　Of the slight figure at the window-pane.

"For me, I loved each lock of shining gold,
　　The dark-hued, violet eyes, the white-rose cheek;
But, more than these, the heart that could enfold
　　A love, whose eloquence no tongue could speak.

"A deep, strange trouble came to me to bear;
　　So dread, death would have been a welcome
　　　　boon;
Dear friends were kind and helpful, and their care
　　Encircled me at night-time and at noon.

" But, in the gloom that gathered fast around,
　　Under the burden of this anguish wild.
I ever shall remember that I found
　　My sweetest solace in a little child.

"A little child, who left her happy play,
　　And nestled in my arms with soothing speech,
Not for a moment, but, through all the day
　　Her tender little ministries would reach.

"Wise as a woman's, were her winsome words.
　　So young in years! So swift to understand!
Most comforting her voice, clear as a bird's,
　　The soft caressing of the dimpled hand."

"Where is she, auntie? Is she living, now?"
　　" My darling, yes—a maiden blithe and fair;
An ardent student, with a thoughtful brow,
　　A dear and choice companion everywhere.

" But never think, because your years are few,
　　You cannot be a real delight and joy;
A loving little helper, leal and true;
　　A faithful worker in a blest employ."

KITTY PENDLETON.

Down where the sun-tipt water comes up to kiss
the shore,
Crowned with a regal glory no proud king ever
wore,
I have found a tricksy fairy, merry, but winsome, too,
Her face as bright as the morning, and eyes of
summer's blue.

Kitty alone in the parlor—(soft! this way, if you
please.)
A quick glance shot through the brown curls,
Nobody hears or sees!   .
Deep in the heart of the ashes burrow plump little
hands,
Laughter low—just hear it!—like gurgle of
brook on the sands.

All over shining ringlets settles the gray-white shower.
What has become of Kitty, left as fair as a
flower?
Where are the dimpled shoulders—where is the rosy
mouth?
And who is this dusk-hued Topsy, fresh from
the sunny South?

And now, demure as a matron, she rocks and soothes
    to its rest
  Her wee little worshipped kitten, held close to
    her loving breast,
Wrapped in a snowy napkin, (I watched through the
    open door)
  Borrowed by dainty fingers from mamma's choic-
    est store.

Then a gush of bird-like music, tender, and sweet
    and clear,
  As she sings to her little nursling, " Hush i
    dear ; hush i *dear !* "
So pretty to see and hear her, our bright-eyed, glad
    little fay !
  God keep the joy on her forehead, for many an
    unborn day.

But dancing feet are quiet as the shadows fall on
    the sea.
  And the low voice, when " Our Father ! " is
    lisped at the mother's knee,
Murmurs, while hasting slumber comes to the baby-
    brain,
  "I happy to see you, mamma ; good night, call
    again."

KITTY'S MISSION.

A little maid, whose summers counted three,
  Came from a joyous visit to an aunt;
Home greetings over, on she danced with glee,
  To seek each dear, familiar, baby-haunt,
While two fond ladies talked of her and smiled,
Watching the graceful pastime of the child.

"Edith," said Auntie Kate, "you must not paint
  Too proud a future for your darling there;
Truly you have small cause to make complaint,
  She is so winsome and so very fair;
But she is slow to learn; she will not be
A scholar, sister, yet, it seems to me,

She is the sweetest, gladdest little one
  I ever knew; each hour and every day,
She warmed and cheered us like a tiny sun,
  Patient, obedient, loving, helpful, gay,
Her work must be, with such a heart and face,
To make the world a brighter, better place."

Aunt Kate was right, in part, and partly wrong,
  Last year I saw that radiant little child
Fresh from class-honors, and, in all the throng
  Of sweet girl-graduates, none fairer smiled;
Yet, 'mid her triumphs, love ruled ever more,
And Kitty shone a sunbeam, as of yore.

CAROLYN.

I sit beside my western window, where
  The gold of sunset gleams
And try to picture in the landscape fair,
  The real and that which seems.

Adown the street, by Casco's flashing tide,
  I see a child at play;
A lovely child, who, yonder, stands a bride,
  In stately grace to day.

Which is the dearer, which the fairer, I
  Can surely never tell;
But this I know, the same sweet virtues high
  In child and woman dwell.

Some lives there are, which, starting free and
    strong,
  In dawn's soft splendor warm,
Run their glad race until the twilight long,
  Untouched by cold, or storm.

God grant such gracious gift to her we love,
    If we may dare to plead,
Aud fill her life with fullness from above,
    Supplying hourly need,

Wisdom and strength for each new duty high
    And patient love through all
And tenderness for souls joy has passed by
    And ruth for suffering's call.

A joyous childhood and a youth content,
    Safe shielded from all wrong ;
And now the crowning grace to life is lent,
    The sweetness to earth's song.

THE OLD CHURCH UNDER THE LEDGE.

This church, the first one built in Yarmouth, then North Yarmouth, Me., was erected in 1729 and its needless destruction about 1835 sent a thrill of indignation through the town that has not ceased to vibrate yet. Built strongly of white oak and occupying a lonely, but lovely spot, not required for any other purpose, it might and should have stood till this time, a quaint and revered relic of the past. The author of "Hester; The Bride of the Islands," makes this old church the scene of the hurried nuptials and Mrs. Elizabeth Oakes Smith pays it a graceful tribute in her story of "The Defeated Life."

Down by the restful Casco, the children find their
   friend.
Kind is the stern-browed giant, faithful to ward and
   defend :

Generous, too, with his bounty, legends of days long
   fled,
Round and round with the seasons, keeping watch
   over the dead.

Passionate Spring-time loves him, and brings with
   their rare perfume,
Garlands of sweet May-blossoms, aglow with their
   dainty bloom.

And the maidens seize their baskets, and follow with
   footsteps fleet,
To gather the fragrant treasures, till weary their
   dancing feet.

Then they toss into odorous masses, the spoils they
    have won away
From the brows of their patient comrade, till he
    hushes their gleesome play,

And they sit on his lap and listen, to his stories of
    Long Ago,
While their young hearts burn within them, and their
    bright eyes overflow,

And they see with their eager vision, through mists
    of time and of tears,
Slowly rising beneath them, the church of a hun -
    dred years !

It stands on the level below them, no marvel of fret-
    work and frieze,
No wealth of cushions and carpets—graces of days
    like these.

No chastened light from its windows, painted with
    rainbow dyes,
But floods of the golden sunshine, straight from the
    vernal skies.

Stanch as the souls that reared it, it looks out over
    the bay,
Silently holding its treasures—tales of an elder
    day—

Memories pure and precious, kept in its watch and
 ward,
Of the men, asleep by the waters, who loved the
 house of the Lord.

Men it is well to forget not, reverent, brave and
 strong,
Worthy the sires they sprang from, honored in story
 and song.

Alden, and Standish, and Brewster, prouder their
 names to-day,
Than title of throned usurper, wrested from ruthless
 fray.

Awed are the worshipping people, grave with the
 danger near,
Lurking ever around them, and the homes they have
 toiled to rear.

To the Gospel of Peace they listen, with bated and
 reverent breath,
Ready to send at a warning, the terrible message of
 death.

But a fairer dawn is breaking, when, fearless of sav
 age blade,
Restful at heart and happy, they come from island
 and glade,

The matron upon her pillion, gay clusters of maidens
    young,
And many a "Little Barefoot," his shoes o'er his
    shoulders flung.

Softly they steal to their places, (the child with his
    wondering air,)
Bringing their grateful tribute—incense of praise
    and prayer.

———

Vanished the old-time vision! leaving but earth and
    sky,
And the young hearts thrilled with their dreaming,
    with a pang, as of one, they cry:—

"The dear old church of our fathers! alas, for man's
    folly and greed!
For the hands that were lifted against it, oh, the pity
    and shame of the deed!

The dear old church of our fathers! Firm it should
    stand to-day,
Telling its quaint old story, to the wee ones tired of
    play,

Teaching its sacred lessons, from pulpit and sound-
    board and wall,
Of the faith and trust of the Christian, and the God
    who is over all."

TO M. D. W.

O friend of treasured days!
    If I could trace in words the wondrous
      scene,
That charmed our sight on Royall's banks of green—
Twilight's rare gift of praise—

If I could only paint—oh, vain!—
The rosy splendor of the sunset sky,
That bent its bright face, where the waters lie,
    'Till the stream blushed again;

Then I might hope, dear heart!
To find fit phrase to syllable for you
The warm regard, the admiration true
    Of life become a part;

And in love's glowing speech,
To breathe the Prayer that all your heart's des r
All good, to which the true soul may aspire,
    Be brought within your reach;

That all the generous care
You grant to other lives, return fourfold
In pure affection's wealth, of price untold,
    To make life blest and fair.

And every volume wise,
That adds to your rejoicing, day by day;
And every tender bud its tribute pay,
    That greets your smiling eyes.

FOR "BROWNIE'S" ALBUM.

M y little friend, how can you bring me here,
  Into the presence of the Poet grand—
Whose stately name is honored far and near—*
  And then ask tribute from my helpless hand!

Dear little Brownie, I would gladly trace
  A shining path for you o'er Life's great sea:
Lift ev'ry shadow from your sunny face,
  And pray your fairest hopes might blossom
    free.

But One, who walks beside you, loves you more
  And in his own good time and perfect way,
Whatever good He takes, He will restore,
  And change the dark'ning night to dawning
    day.

Courage! Press on! Use well your graceful dower,
  The ready brain, the skillful little hand,
The wealth of Fancy and the wondrous power
  All loving, loyal natures e'er command.

Sunshine is sweet, but storm we need, as well;
  We cannot build the soul's fair mansion strong
In joy alone; but pain and sorrow tell
  A deeper story; sing a sweeter song.

*The daring little friend, for whom this was written, reverencing the poet Longfellow, with all her heart, sent him, last spring, a treasure of May-blooms and begged the boon of his illustrious name for her album, which she forwarded. The kindly poet promptly complied with her request and wrote her, besides, a graceful note of thanks for her fresh and beautiful flowers, that carried him back to the woods of Maine and his boyhood.

A GIFT OF POEMS.

DEAR Friend, the world seemed sad and desolate
    ' Mid dark December's chill,
Wanting the light and warmth that emanate
    From joy and hope, and fill

The barren life with bloom and fragrance sweet,
    Though days be cold and drear,
And ring glad music-bells to time the feet
    Of the departing year.

Alone one moment; but the next I stood
    Amid a singing band,
The worshipped ones, the gifted, graceful, good,
    Beloved on sea and land.

O wondrous condescension, that the great,
    Who, crownéd, stand apart,
In genius' shining raiment consecrate,
    Yet love the reverent heart,

And when the shadows gather, softly dim,
    Come with immortal song
And weave their spells, till eyes are all abrim
    With memories buried long.

Tis good to banish for a little space
  Life's bitter loss and pain,
And gather round us all the olden grace
  That may not come again.

My poet-guests sang low, in measures sweet,
  The dear, familiar lays,
While my heart answered with its rythmic beat,
  And poured its eager praise.

Once more within the farmer's *snow-bound* home,
  I feel the ruddy glow,
And share the heartsome comfort of a room
  Quaint with the Long-ago.

The laughing jest I hear, the merry speech,
  The wise and tender tone,
The strange old tales that into marvels reach,
  The voice a world shall own.

What deep, proud joy would fill each noble soul,
  Could the grand future's page
Unroll before them, like a brilliant scroll,
  Its glorious heritage !

But now the *Laureate* sings his silver strain,
  And many a stirring note,
And many a wild and glad and clear refrain
  Over the waters float.

The genial Hood, who, oft, with quaint conceit,
    Moves us to gay surprise,
Breathes out the minor music, rarely sweet,
    Of his sad *"Bridge of Sighs."*

"Mother and Poet!"   Shall we e'er forget
    How the sharp, anguished cry
Rang in our ears?   *Our* eyes were newly wet;
    Our heroes gone to die.

But the home bards are dear beyond compare,
    And sweet will ever be
The liquid song, that sings the city fair,
    That sits beside the sea.

LEILA.

So many paths lie open to your feet,
    Which will you tread?
Which task pursue, till life's work be complete;
    Life's lesson said?

Will you, with deft hand, mould the "plastic clay"
    To beauty's form;
Create, with magic touches, day by day,
    A spirit warm?

Or, will those skillful fingers, bye and bye,
    The rare art know
To paint the tints, that flush the earth and sky
    With radiant glow?

Will you, instead, store up the gold of life,
    To spend again
In thought made strong by the soul's toil and strife,
    Its joy and pain?

Dear child of graceful gifts, choose well your way,
    And make it bright
With pure and high endeavor, till life's day
    Brings rest and night.

BY THE FIRE.

Down in the darkness there twinkles a light
  Jessie is choosing our apples to-night;
Great ruby red ones and golden and green,
  Ripest and sweetest that ever was seen.

Grandmamma sits in her snowy white cap,
  Smiling and smiling her work on her lap,
Looking so dreamy, she's thinking, I know,
  Of happy times vanished, oh, long, long ago.

How the wind whistles! What care we for that?
  Windows may shake and blinds go rat-a-tat;
While we are nestled all cosy and warm,
  Close by the fire, we can laugh at the storm.

Only, don't close all the shutters to-night;
  Some weary man may be cheered by our light;
Some little child may come in and be warm,
  Safe from the bitter wind, safe from the storm.

FAILURE.

I sit in the hush of the autumn eves,
The only season I call my own,
Free from the tyrant of pain, who leaves
The still night hours alone.

Not as I sat in that earlier time
—A wee, odd child, I remember yet—
When the wind rose high in its fitful rhyme,
Or the pane with sleet was wet.

Hasting away from the cheerful board;
From the lights and the pleasant human speech;
For the joy a silent space could afford,
For the bliss a dream could reach.

A dream not of childhood's dear delights,
Of toys and sweetmeats and endless play;
A glimpse of the elf-world's wondrous sights,
That come at the parting day.

But a vision of boundless wealth and power,
Gold that my eager hands should use
To comfort the needy, who, hour by hour,
Brought the plea I would ne'er refuse.

None should suffer that I could aid;
　　None be sad I could soothe, or cheer;
Faltering steps should be kindly stayed,
　　And faint hearts won from fear.

But more than gold I must have one day,
　　Wisdom and knowledge to help my kind;
Food and raiment were well, but they
　　Suffice not the longing mind.

So I would be wise and, with eloquent speech,
　　Uplift the weary to heights afar;
Winning all treasure within my reach,
　　Learning from flower and star.

Ah! days have vanished and years gone by,
　　But where are the lives I have blest and filled,
And where are the hearts, with warm hopes high,
　　Whose sorrows my hand has stilled?

Alas for the noble deeds unwrought!
　　For the kind words breath'd to no list'ning ear;
Alas, for the high dreams come to naught,
　　Ere the autumn of life drew near!

Oh! well for the hopes that are thwarted below,
　　And well for earth's children who falter with
　　　　pain;
The pathway our hesitant footsteps would know,
　　May open in Heaven again.

IN THE SHADOW.

THE summer's fervid heat and glow are past,
  And coming near are the cool, restful days ;
To me they bring no benison, nor cast
  Their bounty on a life attuned to praise.

Yet their sweet advent brings afresh to mind
  How my lost darling ever sought my side,
When, the day's heat and hurry left behind,
  No care could rob us of our eventide.

In shadowed ways my feet had learned to walk,
  Sorrow and Disappointment loved me well,
So well they would not leave me, and their talk
  On my tired sense in lamentation fell.

But through their dirges stole a blithesome strain,
  And happy speech charmed and caressed my ear;
The tender shining that comes after rain
  Brought to my burdened heart content and cheer.

A little form always beside my own,
  A loving hand soft stealing into mine,
How quickly thought on the white forehead shone !
  How flashed the baby wit unique and fine !

My little daughter; close companion; friend!
    I can but linger over days so sweet;
How rare a recompense did Heaven send
    For the strange grief it was my lot to meet!

What joy to me to watch the unfolding mind,
    To learn how rich the treasure in my care!
For her dear sake the past was left behind,
    And Hope lived newly in her promise fair.

Now in my study at the set of sun,
    I wait for the bright face that comes no more,
That cannot come to me till life is done
    And I, at last, reach, safe, the shining shore.

Instinctively I lay my books aside
    To share their choicest wealth with her clear
        mind;
O Death! hast thou the power that can divide
    Two souls whom life has had such strength to
        bind?

BABY'S PICTURE.

THE night is as fair as night can be,
 Rare tint of the sapphire's blue;
And, over the glory, lace-like folds,
 That the azure Heavens shine through.

Was it born of this beauty of sky and cloud,
 The dear, little face I see;
With its dark eyes looking out of a world
 That is white with its purity?

O! beautiful child, with your earnest eyes
 And your thoughtful brow so fair;
Do you come to brighten a little space
 Of this dark earth full of care?

I am tired and worn with the weary way,
 That is fresh to the tiny feet;
But my heart grows glad with a sudden joy,
 At sight of this vision sweet.

So near to God and so near to Heaven
 Is the little life begun;
And so pure is the loving heart that holds
 Praise for the gift of a son!

A heart that is stirred by a tender pain
 For the possible toil and strife,
That wait for the steps of the man to be,
 In this hurrying, struggling life.

For the mother deems that a rougher road
    Leads up from this life below,
For the little lads in their journey through,
    Than our little maidens know. '

Dear heart! If, *ever*, a woman's lot
    Were sheltered, like yours, and sweet ;
If want, and sorrow, and peril dire
    Fled fast from her charméd feet;

If only life's easy, pleasant tasks
    Were set for here hands to do,
And wearisome toil and lonely years
    Were fate of the hapless few;

Then, well might a mother shrink with dread
    From the burdens her son must bear;
For rough, indeed, is the way of life,
    And heavy its weight of care.

Dear friend, be glad for this precious child,
    For the good he will surely share.
And rejoice that a burden of loss and pain
    A merciful fate will spare.

God guide and strengthen the tender feet,
    And hold by the clinging hand,
And lead your darling up to the heights
    Of a goodly, pleasant land!

MY CHRISTMAS CUP.

M y coffee has a flavor rare,
    Now Christmas-tide is overpast;
I give to it no added care,
    That its aroma long should last;
Yet every morning, as I lift
    Your pretty token to my lips,
I gather from the graceful gift
    A sweeter draught than hum-bird sips.

In the clear depths of amber hue
    Two laughing eyes my glances meet;
A fresh, young face as fair to view,
    And, as your English daisies sweet.
A blithesome voice I seem to hear
    In cordial speech and kindly tone,
And echoes gay are dancing near,
    Though I am sitting all alone.

Dear, generous, true-hearted friend,
    As, thus, I drink my portion up,
I pray a loving Hand may send
    All good to mingle in your cup.
Of things that make life sweet to live,
    Noble and pure as it is fair,
May He, who hath all fulness, give
    To you and yours unfailing share.

THE THOUGHTS OF LITTLE MAY.

A fair young mother had dropped earth's care,
    And lay in the midst of summer's bloom,
Her love-lit face and her shining hair,
    Too rare a spoil for the dreary tomb.

Then back, to the stricken home, they brought
    A dear little nestling, turned of four,
Whose soft, dark eyes their shade had caught
    From eyes whose light they would greet no
      more.

The tears fell fast; then the sad voice said,
    As the slight form leaned on the lady's knee,
"Auntie! they told to me—mamma is dead,
    Mamma who loved little Fannie and me."

"Yes, dear, she is dead." "But, auntie, tell,
    Where *is* my mother? I want to see."
"Her happy spirit has gone to dwell
    With Jesus, who said to her, 'Come to me!'

"Her beautiful body lies, at rest,
    In the room where the goldfinch used to sing,
And the snow-white lilies above her breast,
    Are pure and sweet as the breath of spring,

"But the part that loved little May so dear,
    And baby Fannie, has gone, my child,
To God's bright Heaven, where pain nor fear,
    Can reach the home of the undefiled."

"You said that the lilies were on her breast,
    And, now, Aunt Miriam, tell me true,
Her head and feet—are they there, with the rest,
    And her dear, soft hands? Oh, I wish I
        knew!"

'Come and see!" And the small feet softly trod
    The way to the room where the cold form lay.
"Oh, only a *little* has gone to God!
    Auntie, dear auntie, my mamma will stay!"

"Darling! no. That little is more,
    Far, far more than the clay which lies
Pale and still, while the soul will soar
    To joy and rest in the upper skies.

"*She* is not here, and this form she wore,
    We shall lay beneath the 'flowery sod.'"—
"But if *part* of my mother went before
    I must get the rest of her up to God!"

"It may not be. Do not weep, dear one!"
    But the tide of sorrow ran high and strong.
A part to dwell in the joy of the Son,
    And part shut out from the blessed throng!

' Twas a bitter truth for the child to know,
  And hard she found it, to "kiss the rod."
Over and over she murmured, low,
  " I must get my mamma up to God ! "

" We must be patient, my little May,
  For, in God's own time, the forms we love,
He will call from earth, and, in fair array,
  Made pure and bright, they shall live above."

The swe:t face cleared, and the childish speech
  Rose free and glad from the conquered pain,
And she talks of the time, in her thought's far reach,
  " When God shall make mamma over again.'

HER BIRTHDAY.

OH ! to sit in the dark of December,
   And wait for the fall of her feet,
Until, suddenly, I remember
   That the smile, be it ever so sweet,
That passed in the glow of September,
   I never, on earth, shall meet.

But to-day, of all days in the ending
   Of the bitter yet sweet old year,
My fancy is eagerly sending
   Messages far and near,
The past with the present blending,
   Till I dream at length she is here,—

Here, with her arms around me,
   Loving, and warm and white,
The silvery fetters that bound me
   Fast in a world of delight.
Ah, me, that five birthdays have found me
   Wanting the vision bright.

No ringing of happy laughter ;
   No quick little steps on the floor ;
No tapping that follows after,
   Low down on my chamber door,
Till the welcome the night winds waft her,
   Shall bring her to me once more.

So long 'mid the sacred pleasure
   Of angels and sinless men,
Could I clasp her again—my treasure—
   Would her fair face be out of my ken?
Or, by heavenly, as earthly measure,
   Would her five years be grown into ten?

Well I know, did she stand beside me,
   Tho' she came from the bliss of the skies,
I should see, half ready to chide me
   For my sorrow, those radiant eyes,
Whose beauty forever defied me
   To gaze and not thrill with surprise.

And if from the holy splendor,
   She could step over mortal line,
And slip, with its gesture tender,
   Her small, soft hand into mine,
The clasp of her fingers slender
   Would give to me strength like wine.

Oh, my fair little friend, whose graces
    Were a marvel and bliss to my heart,
I must joy, that 'mid love-lighted faces,
    Safe shielded from evil thou art;
That thy birthdays in heavenly places,
    In the rapture of angels have part.

Yet I miss, when the lamp-light is glowing,
    A dear little form from my side,
And the glad, happy speech ever flowing
    On the ear like a musical tide.
My flow'ret in heaven is blowing,
    But on earth it has blossomed and died.

FOR ANNA B. N——.

AMID the tempest—'mid the gloom,
    That stirs our lives, that shrouds our way,
Let us within our souls find room
    For joy that brightens as the day.
For happy thoughts, for gentle deeds,
    That gild the lives of old and young,
Till radiant dawn to night succeeds;
    Or, as the Concord sage hath sung
In guise of prose to reverent friends,
    Writing as only one can write,
Till every sound in music ends,
    And all things glow with lovely light.

APPEAL.

A little shining curl of soft, brown hair,
 The rustle of a loving, long-writ page,
The faint, sad sweetness of a bud once fair,
 Bring back our Golden Age.

Do you recall that sunny autumn time?
 Were ever 'melancholy days' so passing sweet?
Nature forgot the harshness of our clime,
 And walked with gentle feet.

She grudged no gift; she glorified our ways,
 Beauty and balm and happy human hearts—
She sent her warm breath thro' November days,
 Sheathing all cruel darts.

And when the day died in the arms of night,
 Its soul sprang up in flame upon our hearth;
The world shut out, with gay conceit and light,
 We gave the hour to mirth.

Later, when all the laughing echoes slept,
 And the old room grew strangely hushed and
  still,
Around the fire a charméd watch we kept,
 And let thought roam at will.

With what rare cheer one came and blessed us then !
    Would you forget a single golden tone?
Proudly we deemed him peer of noblest men,
    His life not ours alone.

And looking forward saw a future fair,
    In lightning flashes, while with ear attent,
We glowed beneath his words, as unaware,
    He grew so eloquent.

It was too much, I knew it could not last,
    You only smiled, I said it once again,
But we were glad and thought our happy past
    Was worth all future pain.

Ah, me, I do not know ! I read, once more,
    The brave and tender words last penned for
    me,
In drear discomfort, on Potomac's shore,
    And I am brave as he.

But, living over all our saddened years,
    That lay so smiling to our untaught eyes,
I am a coward, and with pain and tears,
    Bewail our sacrifice.

This silence, that has grown between us two,
    Is hard to bear. Shall it not have an end?
Nor time, nor tongue can turn my heart from you,
    I am a loyal friend.

DEPARTURE.

*A*N earnest life has ended upon earth;
  A strong, sweet spirit winged its way to rest;
We talk of death, we mean a nobler birth:
  No doom mysterious, but a lot most blest.

Yet, with dim eyes, that cannot see, for tears,
  The tender hand of Him, who gently led
Our friend belovéd through her saddened years,
  We look around us, seeking what is fled.

Her pain is over, ours but just begun;
  Our loss seems now to us, too sharp to bear;
She will not miss us, she, who was our sun,
  Who warmed and gladdened us with royal care;

But we are poor and desolate and cold
  Without the rare companionship she gave;
How shone the hours with her fine thought's pure
   gold!
  How yearned our hearts to catch her spirit brave!

Not only to our gaze, who loved her so,
  Was it delight to note the graceful mien,
The dark eyes' brilliance, the pale cheek's faint glow,
  Of her we called, in happy days, "Our Queen;"

But friend and stranger felt, alike, the charm
    Of her rare manner and her lovely looks.
Said one, at loss to paint her grace and calm,
    "A woman she, such as we find in books!"

Yet not in beauty's fascinating spell;
    Or, in the costlier gift of mental dower,
Though their united strength we knew so well,
    Lay the sweet secret of her gentle power.

But the warm heart that spent its precious store
    With lavish bounty for the impov'rished soul;
The sunny fortitude with which she bore
    The wreck of fairest hopes; the wise control

Of ardent natures guided by her hand;
    Her eager pressing on to heights above;
Her scorn of wrong—these are they, that command
    Our truest admiration and our love.

O matchless friend, whose life enriched my own;
    Whose presence filled and satisfied my days;
Could I but voice, for thee, in sweeter tone,
    The heart-felt tribute of thy fitting praise!

A LITTLE COMFORTER.

THE year was young, and the year is old,
   But my heart is full of its olden pain.
The fairest flowers their sweets unfold,
The winter's sheen, and the autumn's gold,
   Bring me their treasures in vain.

I miss them so, with their clear, soft eyes,
   And the twining clasp of their dimpled arms,
Their prattling speech, so strangely wise,
Their faces, bright with some glad surprise,
   And all their childish charms!

The year is old, but the year is gay,
   And the cheer and the child-joy everywhere,
Bring back the time, when the festal day
Filled three little hearts, with its brave array,
   As full as they well could bear.

I saw, to-day, on a city street,
   Apart from the hurrying, surging throng,
A wee child, poised on her dainty feet,
Her gold curls tost, but her voice as sweet
   As the words of her little song.

I paused to toy with the golden head,
"I sometimes dance," she nodded and smiled.
"And whose little girl is this?" I said.
"I'm God's little happy Winifred!"
Answered the pretty child.

As I sit, to night, in my room alone,
And only my books and pen for cheer,
The joyous words, with their ringing tone,
As if to conquer the rising moan,
Come back to my listening ear.

The small hand slips into mine, once more,
And the face is fair, though there may not be
The thoughtful look that my darlings wore—
Ah! were they seeking the far-off shore,
That lies o'er the silent sea?

A tiny child! yet she brings a thought
That nestles soft in my aching heart.
A vision oft in my brain has wrought
.My lost ones waiting, in fear, unsought,
Uncomforted and apart—

But murmurs sweet through the stillness flow
"God's happy children!" they seem to say.
"Oh, dear is earth, but never, below,
So warm and tender a love we know,
As brightens our blessed way!"

WEDDING FAVORS.

A summons comes from the west to the east;
  From crowded city, to quiet town ;
"We gather our friends to a marriage feast,
  For we give our daughter—" then, glancing
   down
To learn whom the happy groom may be—
I read with amazement—"W. P!"

Not Baby Walter! It, surely, seems
  But yesterday, or the day before,
His mother and I, with our childish dreams,
  (Together we counted scarce a score,)
Were as busy and happy, at books and play,
As the birds and bees in the month of May.

Dear, little, sunny, rose-cheeked friend !
  Not a hard, or bitter, unloving word,
When life's rich treasure was ours to spend,
  From my winsome playmate I ever heard.
Only fragrant breezes softly blow
Out from that land of my Long Ago,

But another dream and a picture fair
　　Come back to me, as, to-night, I muse,
A blue-eyed boy, with his clustering hair—
　　Once more I glance at the puzzling news—
That wee, small prattler, with mischief rife,
Is he who has chosen himself a wife!

Well, truth is strange, in this world of ours;
　　It must be, that, through childhood's rosy gate,
The baby passed, with his gathered flowers,
　　Into manhood's noble and broad estate.
May he prove it a generous heritage,
A boon and a blessing from youth to age!

And this pearl he has found in his new domain,
　　The crowning grace to a manly life,
May its soft light cheer him in sun and rain,
　　While loving husband and cherished wife
Rejoice that, through pleasant and stormy weather,
They have chosen to walk earth's ways together.

THE PHOTOGRAPH.

Oh, the queerest, quaintest things are little children!
    Now exciting us to laughter, now to tears.
Thrilling us, again, with bits of gravest wisdom,
    Like a grandsire, wise with weight of weary years.
Then, as sudden as the lightning, while we shiver
    With the fear that baby's wings are fully grown,
Comes a flash of baby mischief, all aquiver,
    With the merriment that only earth can own.

Grave, or gay, the tiny creatures hold us captive
    With the force of utter earnestness and truth.
Little matters how absurd a dream or fancy,
    Seeming is the very real to artless youth.
This my thought, while listening, lately, much di-
      verted,
    To a little dark-eyed Charlie's prattle gay;
As the childish voice half sung and half asserted
    Baby thoughts that sent all gravity astray.

While I write the joyous face is bright before me,
    And my Charlie's voice rings clear as a silver
    bell :—
"Do you know the people here in Mamma's album?
    Never mind! You see their names I, quick, can
    tell."
One by one the dear-prized leaves reveal their treas-
    ure,
    Yielding promptly to the tiny, ready hand ;
Baby's comments making all a comic pleasure,
    As they fall from sweetest lips in all the land.

By and by, my wee man finds a smiling picture,
    Where the loving hand a little longer stays,
Cherished still, though wanting all its early freshness,
    Constant friend, in truth, of ante-nuptial days !
This, the sage remark I hear, with laughter shaken,
    Was my fault a want of goodness or of grace ?
"Here's a picture of my precious mamma, taken
    When she had, one time, you know—*a dirty face!*"

ANDOVER BELLS.

Written for the Golden Wedding of EMERY and HANNAH (FROST) MERRILL, Andover, Maine, December 11, 1884.

LET the years roll back with swiftness, to the clear
    December night .
Chosen by a youth and maiden for the solemn, nup-
    tial rite,
That shall link their lives together, doubling joy,
    dividing pain,
Making earth to bud and blossom, like an Eden come
    again.
Though the song of bird is quiet and though hushed
    the singing rills, ·
All the air is full of music and the heart with rapture
    thrills,
Though the winter rules around them, lo ! a miracle
    appears;
Frost has vanished, warmed and melted, soft dissolv-
    ed in happy tears.
Pleasant is the picture dawning from the dimness of
    the past;
Dipt in memory's magic mordant, we can hold its
    colors fast.

"Gracious—kind," thus runs the meaning of the
    name the records show,
Given to this little daughter—bride of fifty years ago·
Fitting title, so we deem it, as we watch her standing
    there,
Sweet, yet dignified in bearing; blue-eyed, modest,
    frank and fair;
Earnest, thoughtful, stands she waiting, ready for her
    noble part.
He no idle dreamer loiters, true his aim and strong
    his heart;
Clear of vision, prompt in action, quick to grasp and
    understand;
Reverent, yet trusting boldly to his vigorous right
    hand.
Each, from all the world, has chosen one to honor
    and to love;
One to trust, through all earth's changes, next to Him
    who rules above;
Forward, to the untried future, fearlessly they take
    · their way;
Life no worthless boon to either, Heaven's fair gift,
    each new-born day.
Willing hands they give to labor; helpful hands to
    kindly deeds;
Counsel wise to all who seek it; tender care for
    others' needs.

All large interests engage them, public welfare, holy
    cause;
Staunch supporters of the Gospel, education and the
    laws,
Honored in their generation, loved and trusted far
    and wide,
This the faintly-outlined story of the farmer and his
    bride.

Beautiful for situation, is the home where cluster,
    sweet,
Precious memories of childhood, where so many
    dancing feet
Pattered, on their busy errands, to and fro, through
    every room,
Making music from the dawning, till the evening's
    silver gloom;
Manly sons and graceful daughters grew in strength
    and beauty here,
Loved and guarded, trained and guided, for the fut
    ure coming near;
Early taught in ways of wisdom, then, with blessing
    and with prayer,
Sent out to their wider culture, trusted to a Father's
    care.
How they loved the fragrant meadows, spread be-
    neath the smiling sun;

Fruitful field and shady orchard, where their rosy
    bloom was won ;
Dear the lovely Ellis river, dear the flashing, foaming
    rills ;
Dear, beyond all power of language, Andover's ma-
    jestic hills.
Never, though to lands remotest, it should be their
    lot to roam,
Will they cease to turn, with longing, to this Para-
    dise of home.

But, amid our joyous measures, tender, loving thoughts,
    to-night,
We must give the little treasures, gone so early from
    our sight ;
Parted from their happy circle, tuneful little voices
    still,
Yet we murmur not but yield us, patient to the Father's
    will,
Knowing well He loves and cares for these safe-folded
    lambs in Heaven,
Just as surely as He watches over all the earthly
    seven;
Guards the group beneath the roof-tree and the
    brother far away,
Whose regretted absence shadows the soft sunshine
    of to-day.

Here, among the guests assembled, held in high es.
    teem by right,
Some there are, who gave their God-speed, fifty years
    ago to-night ;
Few they number, for too many have passed on be-
    fore the rest
To the heavenly marriage-supper, Golden Wedding
    of the blest.

Now, while wedding-bells are ringing in our souls
    their mellow chimes
And our hearts stir with emotion, that disdains all
    feeble rhymes,
We would gladly yield our tribute and breathe low
    the fervent prayer,
That, to those, who fondly love them, may this close-
    united pair
Long be spared to cheer and counsel, rounding out
    a useful life
With the joy and rest they merit, noble husband,
    faithful wife.
Sons and daughters rise to bless them, children's
    children love to come
Back with happy song and laughter to the dear, famil-
    iar home.
Out from this fair homestead going, wide and strong
    a current flows ;

Who can tell how far it reaches; who its priceless
    value knows?
Fifty years of faithful living, this is wealth to hold in
    fee;
Men and women, nobly nurtured, goodly is the sight
    to see!
Such the lives, true and uplifting, justly held a coun-
    try's pride,
Reverent Hail and Farewell! give we, to this farmer
    and his bride.

BABY'S DILEMMA.

A precious baby-boy, just lisping sweet,
  The stubborn accents of our English tongue,
Prayed for a boon not deemed exactly meet,
  By Grandmamma, who o'er his cradle hung.
She called his prattle sweetest in the land ;
  Yet thought it wisest not to understand !

The pretty child looked up in pained dismay,
  His little face a study to behold ;
Grandma deny, who kissed him every day,
  And held him dearer far than gems, or gold?
It could not be ! The fault was all his own ;
  " Ebbie can't talk !" he said in piteous tone.

Ah, baby dear ! Thy artless cause is won.
  Grandma's warm heart is smitten through and
      through ;
Three little trusting words have quickly done
  What rain of passion's tears could never do.
With prayer fulfilled, the little one is blest ;
  And so we leave him to his rosy rest.

ALBUM LINES.

*A*LL ye, who love a soul sincere and true ;
　　Who kinship claim with hearts of generous
　　　mold ;
Who the quick sympathy of friend e'er knew,
　　Write on these pages fair in words of gold.
Write for the joy of one, who *lives* the truth ;
　　Who holds a helpful hand to Sorrow's child ;
Who gives her tenderness to age and youth,
　　Whose way leads upward to the Undefiled.

HELEN'S BABIES.

WHY, yes, it must be many years,
　　But seems as yesterday,
Since Nellie was my pupil, dears,
　　The graceful little fay!

Her blue eyes brimmed with laughing light;
　　Her soft cheek was aglow;
Her gold curls fell, a lovely sight,
　　Around a brow of snow.

As merry as a tricksy elf,
　　This charming, blue-eyed Nell,
It must be of her pretty self
　　They still their stories tell.

Yet this is what I seem to hear;
　　They said, by Southern waters,
Lived happy Nellie and two dear,
　　Delicious little daughters!

These babies had been early taught
　　To bow, in reverent mood,
When their papa God's blessing sought
　　Upon their daily food.

The tiny sprites had journeyed far.
  To the New England home,
Where sported once that child-mamma,
  Down by the salt sea foam.

At morning meal the scene was new
  And bright eyes roamed, it may be ;
So Bessie, when the grace was through,
  Had this to say to Baby :—

" You did not bow your head, my dear,"
  She spoke in accents sober,
" When Papa prayed." 'Twas very clear,
  Her life reached late October !

" If *Bessie's* eyes were shut up *well*,"
  The baby archly said,
" I do not see how she could tell,
  I did not bow my head !"

CORA—A DAUGHTER.

RIEF and pretty title ;
   Full of meaning, too.
Do you know, I wonder,
   All it tells of you ?

Like a perfect poem;
   Like the song of bird ;
So much pleasant music
   In a single word !

Sweet to be a "daughter,"
   In a sheltered home ;
Needing not, nor caring,
   Yet awhile to roam ;

Cherished and enfolded
   By the purest love,
God has sent to show us
   What is Heaven above.

Gentle duties wait you,
   Every day and hour ;
Graceful duties, making
   Life a fragrant flower,

Yielding truest pleasure
  For your tender thought,
Into loving service
  Reverently wrought.

So I count you happy
  In your girlhood free ;
Make the present noble;
  Let the future be.

If a deeper gladness,
  If a wider life,
Should await your coming ;
  Or a sadder strife,

You will joy or suffer,
  With a truer heart,
If, as faithful daughter,
  You have borne your part.

SEVEN YEARS.

OH, these nights in the young September!
    Autumn's coolness on summer's glow—
Sitting here, how can I but remember
    All the charm of the Long Ago?
Flashes a face from the moonlight's shimmer,
    Flushed with the tinting of shells on the
        beach,
Dark grey eyes that are bright with the glimmer
    Of thoughts that shall dawn into noble
        speech.

Vanished the years, and I stand beside you,
    Where the waters come up to the shore,
Proud that no regal gift is denied you,
    Eager to gather the Future's store.
Little I pause for your smile at my dreaming,
    Well I interpret your lip's decree;
"On, like that highway of fairy-light streaming,
    Shall be your path o'er life's wonderful sea."

I spoke with a thrill, but I knew not how truly.
    How should I see the red phantom afar?
Only to broaden the triumphs then newly
    Won by your conflicts at desk and at bar—

This my sole thought as the glad weeks went
    by us,
  Never a dream of the perilous strife,
Never a vision of all to come nigh us,
    When guilty hands threatened the nation's
    life.

Yet the day came, and then, clear—without falter,
  Rang out your voice with its clarion call,
"Down with the foe who has dared to assault her,
  Dear-beloved land that has cherished us all!"
Who could resist all that manly appealing?
  Was it a marvel men gathered in crowds?
"Oh! it is grand, how these days are revealing
  Souls that untroubled prosperity shrouds."

Well, you could say it, but had you not come to
    them,
  Would they have roused into action sublime?
Might not the voice of the Great Need been
    dumb to them,
  Wanting your touch in that terrible time?
Warm from the heart came the truth and the
    pleading,
  Not a "Go thou," but a frank "Come with
    me;"
Strong and yet loving the hand that was leading
  Whithersoever the danger might be.

Bright and brief as that sea-track of splendor,
 Swept a brave life to its patriot close.
"Shot—through the heart—one more gallant
  defender,"
 Flashed the sharp news from the home of
  our foes.
Then—well, what then? When a blow like that
  falls on us,
 Shivers, to fragments, Life's beautiful dream ;
Only—the stern voice of Duty still calls on us,
 Days must go on, though they wearisome
  seem.

Yet, as I sit, mid the hush and the glory,
 Stirred out of calm by the loss and the pain,
In fancy I sketch the impossible story,
 As though the old brightness were round
  me again.
Ah ! nevermore here—but beyond these sad
  changes,
 I know a grand spirit still soars and aspires,
With God-given scope for the mind as it ranges,
 And blessed content for the warm heart's
  desires.

CLARA—BRIGHT; ILLUSTRIOUS.

PROUD is the title ; yet, at thought of thee,
 A brief line haunts me like a sweet refrain ;
It paints more truly, so it seems to me,
 And is, " Like the clear shining, after rain."

Better than fame are the clear words of truth ;
 Better the life one liveth, free from stain.
Then, ever be, as in thy gladsome youth,
 Like the soft splendor that comes after rain.

WRITTEN IN AN ALBUM.

IF thou would'st lift thy friends to lofty heights,
 Expect from each the best that each can do;
For trust in man, his noblest power excites
 And helps him on to all things just and true.

A QUESTION.

Bot that I never wondered before,
But on that morning I wondered more,
What little boys' heads were made of;
The snow had come like a vision of night,
Soft and silent and dazzlingly white,
Like Floy's dream-city of Nadov.

Then up, with the earliest beams of the sun,
Rose Paul and Tommy and every one
Unscared by the winter weather;
Such a din, as they muffled and capeied and sang,
Then a jubilant shout through the whole house rang,
As they all trooped off together.

I quickly parted my curtains to see
What the sudden joy of the boys could be,
And held my breath in amazement!
A high-topped wall they had gained with a bound
And under it lay a feathery mound,
Not far away from my casement.

Up mounted a trio with deafening sound,
While two laddies stood below on the ground,
I wondered why for a minute;
Then three little forms shot swift through the air
Heads downward, vanishing, where, O, where?
"The snow-mound," cried Floy, "they're in it."

All but the six, small, quivering feet,
"They will break their necks!" I sprang from my seat;
    "A crazier thing was, never!"
But that *corps de reserve*, all ready to act,
Drew out the dear little fellows intact,
    As rosy and sound as ever.

Now a daring leap is a glorious thing
And so is a sky-ascending swing
    Rare joy amid joys bucolic;
But a reckless venture, it seems to me
With a head for a battering-ram, you see,
    Is a dangerous kind of frolic.

Yet the boys went on in their heedless play,
(I thought that one e would be changed to a)
    And still not a woe befell them;
So when people ask as they've asked before,
What heads are made of, I say it is more,
    Much more than I ever can tell them.

SONG—MARGARET.

come to me with thy presence bright !
  I wait for thee, I have waited long ;
O let me thrill with the old delight
  Of thy dreamy and tender song !
The day is gone with its darkness drear ;
  The night blooms out like a lily sweet ;
O come to me, I am waiting here
  For the sound of thy footsteps fleet.

The night blooms out like a lily fair
  Agleam with its chrismal bath of dew ;
Its soft light falls on thy golden hair
  And a face that the soul shines through ;
A rare, sweet face with its tender glow,
  That stirs my heart to its olden pain ;
O come with the smile that I used to know
  And thy low voice's clear refrain.

A soft breeze stirs in the leafy bowers,
  A light step quickens my pulse's beat ;
It is she, the fairest among the flowers,
  As stately and calm and sweet ;
But the rose hue burns on her cheek of snow,
  As I gather the small hand closer yet ;
She is mine, as in days of the long ago,
  O my pearl, O my Margaret !

TREASURES.

OUR frolicsome band of three—
   Bertie and Ralph and John—
As pretty a group to see
   As ever the sun shone on.

Bertie, with dark blue eyes,
   And hair in clustering curls,
A face that a painter would prize,
   Thoughtful and fair as a girl's.

His quaint little sayings bring,
   (So winsome and strange and wise,)
Sometimes our laughter's ring,
   And sometimes tears to our eyes.

Jackie, as blithesome and free
   As lambs that skip on the hills,
A voice that is sweet to me,
   And soothes like murmur of rills.

Pale little rings of gold
   Lie on his forehead white,
Gayest one of the fold,
   Blue eyes dancing with light.

Tiny, but graceful and strong,
  Speeding like bird from view ;
No height where his hands belong,
  But feet must follow too.

Brimming over with glee,
  Never two moments at rest,
Save when the sunbeams flee,
  And he seeks his cosy nest.

Baby Ralph closing the list,
  Blue-eyed, too, like the others,
Doubling his plump little fist,
  Laughs and applauds his brothers ;

Longing, no doubt, for the day
  Of wonderful strength like theirs,
When he shall gambol and play,
  Unawed by mountains of stairs.

Our frolicsome band of three,—
  Bertie and Ralph and John,—
As pretty a group to see
  As ever the sun shone on.

DESIDERANS FINEM.

I come, once more, into my little room.
　Ended is every weary, bitter task.
Welcome to heart and brain the gathering gloom;
　What sweet relief to throw aside this mask!

My pretty room! How bright it used to glow,
　How filled with sunny presence all day long,
What waves of gladness, in their golden flow,
　Broke from my happy heart in grateful song!

I could not bear to cloud their beaming way,
　To cast the shadow of my woe across
Their joyous brows, and darken all the day
　With sad reminders of my heavy loss;

And so I strove to call a sound of cheer
　Into the voice that only longed to moan,
To make the sunshine in my eyes appear
　And summon smiles the wrung heart must disown.

To do, with all the strength I could command,
　What best would help and comfort them, I thought,
To hold my heart down with a forceful hand—
　Alas, how worse than vainly have I wrought!

"How well she looks, how lightly sits her grief!
  I thought her speech more sorrow would reveal.
'Tis strange, how soon the sick heart finds relief,
  But there *are* they, who cannot deeply feel."

Even the loving little boy, who bears
  That precious, precious name, reproachful, said,
Gazing upon me with fast-coming tears,
  "Have you *forgotten* that my uncle's dead?"

O God, it is too much! What can I do?
  Help me to bear this added anguish now.
Why must they cut my sore soul through and through?
  Why press the thorns into my bleeding brow?

I've stood with him upon the vessel's deck
  He'd trod so often in his manly pride,
When every moment threatened it a wreck,
  Father, if then, together, we had died!

Again, in peril on far Southern seas,
  The dark death-angel brought his message low.
The tempest touched me, light as summer breeze,
  My soul made answer, "It is sweet to go."

Oh, had it been! Then all these pangs were o'er.
  A grave with him beneath those wondrous skies,
A home with him upon that radiant shore,
  Where, from blest hearts, immortal praises rise.

In the thick gloom through which my feet must tread,
  My eyes have strengthened, so that I can see.
I know, now, what earth means without my dead,
  Life is not life, nor is death death to me.

Let me not weakly murmur.   Be my stay,
  O Lord, the Merciful, as well as Just!
Keep me from fainting in my joyless way,
  Till the sweet words are uttered, "Dust to dust."

I sue for patient strength to bear my cross,
  Till, in Thy view, Thy holy will is done;
To bear these stinging thrusts—my being's loss,
  Till thou shalt crown me with my being's sun.

COMFORTED.

The incident on which the following poem is founded—and which took place many years ago in a town near Auburn—was related to me by a friend as follows: "A lady had died leaving two little children who were at once adopted into another home. The little ones mourned greatly over their loss, and could not be comforted. On one occasion they were weeping bitterly, after they had been left for the night, when the family were suddenly startled by hearing the mother's voice—which was perfectly familiar to them all— speaking in soothing tones to the little creatures, who presently hushed their sobbing and went quietly to sleep. In the morning mention was made to the children of their crying the night before 'Yes' said one, 'we *did* cry till mother came and got us to sleep.' The affair caused no little excitement at the time, in the town where it occurred, and to this day, in speaking of it, people can only say, 'what a singular thing it was that happened to those children!' To me the circumstance seems as touching and beautiful as it is strange."

IN the midst of the glory of autumn time,
   When the world was aflush with the wondrous light
That slips from the red man's blessed clime,
   Ere the year goes out in night,

Two pale hands threaded the clustered gold
   That nestled close to the mother's heart;
Ah, sharp is the sorrow the moments hold
   With dear lives drifting apart!

One long, long kiss, that must be the last.
   "Grieve not, my darlings! If God above
Be the God I worship, then—hold this fast—
   I will comfort you still with love."

Fair, so fair in her dreamless rest!
  Fragrant flowers on her bosom's snow;
Why this anguish He knoweth best,
  Whose just hand dealeth the blow.

Gentle the accents that strive to cheer
  The stricken babes in their lone estate;
But the wee ones yearn for the lost and dear
  Who has left them desolate.

At night as they wept in their tiny bed,
  Gold curls mingling with curls of jet,
"Sad little creatures!" a maiden said,
  "Their sore hearts cannot forget."

"Hark!" said another, "I hear her call!"
  And soft through the silence, the mother's voice
Floats with a music that stirs them all
  To wonder and yet rejoice.

A tender music of loving speech;
  Low, sweet words like a lullaby,
Soothing murmurs the listeners reach,
  And a breath like a human sigh.

A startled group by the parlor fire,
  With strange amaze in their speaking eyes;
But the children, granted their hearts' desire,
  Quiet their grieving cries.

"You wept last night!" As the lady said,
  She folded the lovely pair to her breast,
"We wept until mother came close to our bed,
  And soothed us into our rest;

"She was bright and fair as the angels are;
  We saw her face in the darkened room
For the dear, dear voice that had seemed so far,
  Carried away the gloom.

" She kissed us both, and we felt no fear;
  And she talked so sweet, till the pain was gone;
Then the first we knew, you were standing here,
  And the beautiful day was born."

WEE MARGARET.

Winsome little Margaret,
    Tell me, are you ready yet?
I am waiting with my sled,
New and bright and painted red,
It will bear you like a queen,
Dainty little Daisy Deane.

Pretty little Margaret,
Did you think I could forget?
Come, the air is crisp and clear,
Boys are coasting far and near,
We'll outshine them all, my pet,—
Dark-eyed little Margaret.

Laughing little Margaret,
Here she comes with curls of jet,
Eyes alight and cheeks aglow,
Like two roses in the snow,
Precious little roll of fur,
Who has seen the like of her?

Look, dear Baby Margaret,
See your name in gold is set,
On each side my handsome sled.
It was done by Uncle Ned.
Now we're ready, off we go,
Dashing, flashing o'er the snow.

JESSIE'S PROSPECT.

DARK-EYED little Jessie
   Stood beside my chair;
Bright her eager face was,
   Free from every care;

Sweet her clear voice sounded
   As she murmured low,
" I will tell you, something,
   That you'd like to know.

"My mamma has bought a
   Cape so soft and warm,
Made of fur to keep her
   Safe from cold and storm.

"Now, you see, when she has
   Grown so young and small,
That she cannot wear it,
   Any more at all,

"I shall be a woman,"
   Said the little elf,
"And the pretty fur cape,
   I can wear myself."

CHARLIE'S HARP.

A dear little fellow lives down on my street,
 As happy a lad as you ever would meet,
If you traversed our Uncle's dominions ;
A kind little heart that does good when it can,
But, though he is such a mere dot of a man,
 As firm as a rock, his opinions.

One day he was ill from a "terrible cold ;"
So he took up a harp that a trader had sold
 Him at Christmas for dear brother Tom ;
"I want one just like it," he said to a friend,
Who had dropped in an hour with the captive to
  spend,
 "But you know I must stay where 'tis warm,"

So I wish you would buy me a harp just like this ;
I've got some more money to give Mr. Bliss,
 It takes only eight cents to buy it."
Off went Master Harry, as grand as a lord,
His money held fast under close watch and ward,
 As he thought, Charlie says, "I shall try it."

In a very few moments young Harry came back,
And drew from the depths of his bright-buttoned
    sacque
  A tiny harp wrapped all. in paper ;
" I paid only six cents ; the others were ten,"
" Dear me ! who'd have thought it ? " up sprang
    Charlie, then,
  " How dare he serve me such a caper ? "

The cold was forgotten ; on went his surtout,
And he cried, as he stood in one slipper, one boot;—
  " He shall never cheat me in that fashion !
I paid only eight cents.   Come, Harry, don't laugh!"
For, in his excitement, instead of his scarf,
  He had tied little Vinnie's red sash on.

"Well, what can I do for you, Charlie, my lad,"
"I want a big harp just like what Tommy had,
  And I've brought back this poor little, mean one
I paid to you five cents—and one cent—and two ;
I counted them over, I know it is true,
  And I'll take, if you please, a big, green one."

" Very well, if you pay me the four cents beside,"
The trinket was tempting, the boy sorely tried,
  But he could not give in to *extortion.*
" It isn't the money I'm thinking about,"
He said to the man, as he turned to go out,
  With this—for result of his caution ;—

His six precious pennies he carried once more ;
For " I will give two, but I cannot give four,"
   He resolved, and the harp left behind him.
God grant little Charlie as firmly may stand,
For the *truth*, and the *right*, and as prompt be his
     hand,
   When sin, or temptation would bind him !

NELLIE'S OPINION.

"THE merriest people are best, I know,"
  Said wise little blue-eyed Nell,
As we all sat watching the fire-light glow,
  While the evening shadows fell.

"The merriest folks are the best, I know;
  For those who are laughing and gay
Are the ones who are willing to stop and show
  Tired people an easier way.

"There is Harry Brown, with his mischievous face,
  That never is sober an hour;
He's always ready to yield his place
  To poor little Catharine Tower,

"For Katie has ever so far to walk,
  And her clothing is scanty and thin;
And Harry, he hushes the boy's rude talk,
  And lets little Katie come in.

"To-day, as we came home from school, mamma,
  Past the brook and the little run,
We saw foolish Bessie, and young Mr. Carr,
  Who is always so full of his fun.

" But his face was as gentle as gentle can be,
　　Because of her trouble and pain.
She had slipped on the ice, and her basket, you see,
　　She had lost, nor could find it again.

"Now stiff Mrs. Decker and Clarissa Bray,
　　With that solemn-faced Joshua Hyde,
Who thinks it is sinful to laugh—well, *they*
　　Passed her by, on the other side.

" But young Mr. Carr, with his pleasant face,
　　Gave poor silly Bessie his arm,
And led her along to an easier place,
　　With the basket he'd saved from harm.

" So the merriest people are best, I think ;
　　And if I were hungry and poor,
I should just go ask for my food and drink
　　Of the smiling folks, I am sure."

THE MEETING-HOUSE ON THE HILL.

The following stanzas were suggested by a late plan to form an association for the preservation of the old Baptist church in Yarmouth, Maine. This church, which was erected in 1797, has been only recently vacated by the society for a more centrally located site. It is proposed to convert the building into a reading room and antiquarian hall for the preservation of relics, of which there are many in the old town and to use the house for a place of pleasant entertainment for old and young. This idea owes its inception to the active brain of Mrs. George W. Hammond, whose generous heart and ready hand are incessantly occupied in plans for the improvement of the village, in which she has recently made her home. It is hoped that the children of the church, and of the town wherever they may be, will kindly aid in the carrying out of this praiseworthy enterprise.

WE blame our sires for a ruthless deed,
  That swept from the earth away
The quaint old church, where, in fear and need,
  The people came to pray.

Where they sought, though with peril on every side,
  The help of the God on high,
And, strong in the strength of their guard and guide,
  Stood ready, at call, to die.

Our hearts are stirred by the story old,
  Which is still forever new
And we spare no words, as the scenes unfold,
  That open the past to view.

Shall we work such ill as our fathers wrought
 And the Vandal hand again
Be lifted against a church dear-bought
 At cost of toil and pain?

The cherished church, that has welcomed long
 The seeker after truth
And summoned to battle against the wrong,
 Manhood and age and youth?

Can we claim no spot in this ancient town,
 Where the children, that yet, shall be,
May come and, with reverent heads bowed down,
 The storied days may see?

No roof that has echoed the fervent prayer
 That parted the solemn gloom,
The praise of a Father's love and care,
 That rang through the lofty room?

We can spare it not. Let the old church stand
 At the head of its quiet street;
Let us guard its walls with a loving hand
 And bring to it blossoms sweet;

Make it fair and pleasant to old and young
 And fill it with light and cheer;
Let the page be read and the song be sung,
 That gladden the wintry year.

Let us bring to it relics of days gone by,
    Our treasures from over the sea;
The stores of the past, that no gold can buy,
    The pride of our birth-land free.

Let the old church stand on its goodly site,
    Made beautiful as we will;
A trust from the old-time men of might,
    Our Meeting-house on the hill!

ON THE TENTH ANNIVERSARY OF A FRIEND'S MARRIAGE.

DEAR friends, in this blank envelope please find
   Congratulations for the years behind,
With wishes warm that a new decade prove
A shining path rayed round with peace and love;

Continual comfort in the little man,
Whose happy life as valentine began;
Blessing and honor from the sad hearts cheered
By your sweet, generous lives; from all endeared

By ties of kinship, or of culture, may
Rare pleasure crown you on your wedding-day.
Out from the dark I send this little prayer—
God's gracious gifts go with you everywhere.

ESTELLE.

ANOTHER golden season dropped away
  Into the past.
I count its moments through this April day,
  And hold them fast;
Wishing their presence, sweet as latter May,
  Might longer last.

You bring to me, like matchless days in June,
  Brightness and calm;
And from a nature wondrously in tune,
  My sad thoughts arm
With cheerful courage, as with strength of noon
  And hope like balm.

I listen to the melody that slips
  From your skilled touch,
The magic of those slender finger tips,
  Nor wonder much
The harmony in life, as on the lips,
  Is ever such.

Tis good, oh friend of many gifts, to see
　　A fine, fair face,
And know a mirror true 'twill ever be
　　Of the soul's grace,
The mind's high nature that bids folly flee,
　　Gives virtue place.

I linger over hours that you have made
　　Bright, sweet and strong,
And mourn the debt has been so ill-repaid
　　Of blessed song,
Of sympathy, whose memory will not fade,
　　Though life last long.

And in these years that have swept slowly by,
　　The shadow fell
Upon your perfect days, from cloudless sky.
　　You heard the knell
Of loving hopes, and yet you patient cry :—
　　" I know 'tis well! "

While you look back upon the sunlit past,
　　And feel the glow
Of the great love, that, sure, in heaven must last,
　　It cherished so,
The friend on whom so many hopes were cast,
　　Sweet years ago !

Whatever joy the future has in store,
    Whatever pain ;
If we at length, reach safe the shining shore,
    Where Love doth reign,
It will be well, though we were wounded sore,
    Such peace to gain.

IN MEMORIAM.

T. G. C.

A fairer home than earth
   Claims heart of noblest birth;
His duties bravely done,
An early crown is won
And he, whose death we mourn,
To fuller life is borne.

M. D. C.

A little life begun;
One little glad note sung;
Then rest and joy in Heaven
And tender nurture given;
Sweet, with the Father's love,
The full strain flows above.

J. C. S.

She wrought with tireless hand
To guard her little band
And loyal sons to-day
Their grateful tribute pay;
Loss, grief and pain are past
And Heaven is her's, at last,

C. T. C.

He walks the streets he longed to see;
  He hears the music of his dreams;
The truth he sought with ardor,'he
  Reads plain beside Heaven's crystal
    streams.

A. L. D.

She was our treasure, yet we leave her here
  And go our way without her love and
    light;
Trusting to see, when sight has grown more
    clear,
  Why day's soft glory changed to moonless
    night.

ETHELIND.

I have never told you of Ethelind,
    But you weary so of your burden, child,
And you droop so sore under grief's cold wind,
    While your blue eyes gather a look so wild,
It may rest and strengthen your heart to-night,
    To hear of a brave little girl I knew
Many years agone, with an eye of light
    And a soul that was fashioned of spirit and dew.

Not a faultless form, not a perfect face,
    Though the first was slender and lithesome, too
And the last was full of the nameless grace,
    That the soul sends out to the keen eye's view;
Not a shining curl, but the smooth hair swept
    Back from a brow that was pale with pain;
Not a rose-bud mouth where the dimples slept
    And waited for love to make them again,

But power in the firm lip's quick control
    And swift, from the depths of the wondrous eye,
Came the flash of a beauty and strength of soul
    Earth's richest argosy could not buy;

Eyes all too large for a face so thin,
    Yet they thrilled me and held me, like a spell,
So earnest and pure from the life within ;
    So brimmed with a meaning no words could tell.

Such a wee, strange child, so daintily neat;
    The small hands so faithfully ply their task,
While the play-ground echoes to little feet
    And her truant mates in the sunshine bask ;
But the dark eyes love to wander away
    To the woods and rocks and the sounding shore
And, at twilight, her fancy gone astray,
    Hears the shadows trooping from hill and moor·

Oh, why do you look at me so, dear child?
    I am sketching no saintly maiden now,
But a girl with a nature deep and wild
    And a soul undaunted, that could not bow.
They called her arrogant, haughty and cold
    As she passed on lightly adown the years,
Too grave and stern, I was sometimes told,
    Unmoved as little by smiles, as tears.

Perhaps.   But she never from truth would part;
    A hater of shams from her inmost soul;
Cold?   Then is the volcano's molten heart
    As frigid as ice at the wintry pole ;

At war with the tyrant of pain, from her birth,
   Such pain as would conquer a giant's strength ;
Small leisure was left her for careless mirth,
   Yet she wrought with the will that must conquer
     at length.

No genius was hers with a lofty flight,
   Mounting at ease from the mists and pain,
But wearisome toil up the shining height
   And delving for treasure, grain by grain.
No gifted mistress of matchless song,
   Though her voice held music most strangely
     sweet,
Not an eloquent lip, but thoughts would throng
   And glow from the dark eyes calm retreat.

Little May, can you catch, from my impotent tongue,
   Some sense of this nature, so proud, so strong?
Could it bear, do you think, its great love flung
   Back from a false heart it had trusted long?
No quivering lip and no drooping eye,
   While scorn lay so deep it could not be read;
Not a thought turned back from her purpose high
   By the rising moan over gladness fled.

And the years brought joy that was sweet and strange,
   The priceless wealth of a manly heart;
The strong, true love that could know no change
   Though fate should lead ever their lives apart.

Rich-dowered with his kingly gifts, he stood,
    And eager to battle for truth and right;
No—not for this life—was that radiant good,
    Death's darksome billows whelmed all in night.

At the lucent depths of those changeful eyes,
    Forever a haunting anguish lay;
No more, glad songs from her heart would rise,
    Yet the brave soul kept on its steadfast way;
A quiver of pain in the sweet voice's tone,
    But, from strength to strength, till her feet
        should stand
Above the steeps of this earthly zone
    Unfettered and free in the Fatherland.

WITH A LITTLE GIFT.

DEAR Sue, I send a tiny harp
  With love's own music in it;
If I could write that music out,
  How gladly I'd begin it.

But when your skilful fingers touch
  The little shining token,
Perhaps 'twill sing, itself, the words
  Not easy penned or spoken.

And you may know these slender strings
  (So slight, yet so enduring,)
Are loving thoughts that link us two,
  All mem'ries sweet ensuring,

And that the golden-silken band,
  That holds them in connection,
No purer is, or stronger than,
  The bond of true affection,

Go, little harp, and breathe your lay
  In love's most tuneful numbers;
Go, waken happy thoughts, by day,
  And soothe her to her slumbers.

THE MOTHER'S LULLABY.

SWEET is the hour that lures each little ranger
    Back to the charms of the happy home-nest;
Proudly recounted each exploit and danger,
    Baby griefs wept out on pitying breast.
Holy the vision of childish forms kneeling—
    Smile though we may, little maid, little man!—
"Please fordive Harry," thus runs the appealing,
    "And all of the rest of us, too if you tan!"

Quaint little orisons, soon they are over,
    Rosy lips sealed with the comforting kiss;
Silently slumbers the tired little rover,
    Earth hath no scene that is purer than this.
Low droops the mother's fair head o'er her treasures;
    "Father! oh guide them, oh, keep them from
        harm;
Grant them—far more than the world's choicest
        pleasures—
    Infinite love and the strength of Thine arm!"

Two little tender forms, weary with weeping,
　　Two little aching hearts wounded and sore;
Two little orphans, who, waking or sleeping,
　　Yearn for the footsteps that echo no more.
Two golden heads on one pillow are lying,
　　Soft, rounded cheek and long eyelashes wet;
Loving arms linked 'mid their sorrowful crying,
　　Sad little mourners, they cannot forget!

Hark! through the night-tide low music is stealing;
　　Brightens the gloom to wide, wondering eyes,
Vision of joy to their glad sight revealing
　　Dear-beloved form in its angel-disguise.
Eager they gaze—there can be no mistaking—
　　Sweet mother-tones are caressing the ear;
Smiles, like the dawn from the dark tempest breaking,
　　Bring to the stricken babes comfort and cheer.

Touch, light as down, upon lovely brow lingers;
　　Thrills the young heart with an exquisite peace;
Soothed by the chrism of love-freighted fingers,
　　Sorrow and sobbing grow fainter and cease.
Slowly fringed eyelids droop over the gladness
　　Throned in blue eyes that knew only to weep;
Sweet lips, forgetting their burden of sadness,
　　Falls now the soft benediction of sleep.

A QUARTETTE.

HAVE you heard of the birds, little Ethel,
    That live in the warm south land?
Some are of glittering plumage
    And some are a strange-voiced band;

But the oddest of all, I fancy,
    Are the birds that have won their name
From the quaint little words they utter,
    And the words are always the same.

Close down by your door sits a birdie
    And cries, as you come into view;
Or he calls, quite near, if you're walking,
    "Who are you? who-who-who are you?"

Another, wise little songster,
    Bids you cheerily all the day,
Whether you're going, or coming,
    "Work away, work-work-work away!"

A third little, sorrowful singer,
  In his queer, little notes of woe,
Wails out his pitiful pleading,
  " Willie, Willie, come go ; come go ! "

And, far away up the country,
  A fourth, you have heard of him, still
His place is here with the others, yes,
  'Tis the Whippoorwill, " Whip-poor-Will."

HIS LAST.

WHAT shall we do with our darling, our baby?
   Winsome and sweet, but so full of his pranks;
If you can tell us, one dear little lady
   Will owe you her truest and heartiest thanks.

Listen! This morning, though rain-drops were falling
   Into the town must ride little mamma;
"Overshoes, dearie!" came grandmamma, calling,
   "Close by the door that is left just ajar."

Little mamma looked in vain all about her;
   Wardrobe, nor hall would the secret confess;
Gone were the overshoes, no one could doubt her;
   Where they had hid themselves, no one could
      guess.

Hid themselves! Ah, when the noon is advancing
   And the good grandmother lays her neat board;
What an odd light in her dark eyes is dancing,
   As she peeps in where her light loaves are stored!

There, on the fragrant mounds, there are the missing
    ones!
  Oh, such a baby! Now what can we do?
Shall we be chiding ones, shall we be kissing ones?
  Say, little Linda, which, if it were you?

THE OLD ALBUM.

HERE, in the midst of the jubilant joy
　　Born of the beauty of earth and sky,
I turn, with a thrill, to the old employ,
That claimed its tribute from maiden and boy,
　　In the sweet years long gone by.

For lo ! as I softly rustle the leaves,
　　Fragrant, yet, with the young heart's prayer,
A sacred trio my sight receives,
And thought that gladdens, and thought that grieves,
　　Awake with the music there.

One sings of eternity's "Peace or Pain,"
　　And "None But Christ," is another's thought;
While the third brings back, with his pleasant strain,
The earnest voice in the holy fane,
　　That Sabbath on Sabbath brought.

Sweet to recall, with their gifts and grace,
    The faithful guides to our young lives given,
Though gone from our vision each well-loved face,
Two called higher to earthly place,
    And one called higher—to Heaven.

Sure, not in vain were you daintily wrought,
    Little volume in scarlet and gold !
Since, through the years with their changes fraught,
Blessing, like this, you have silently brought,
    Treasure that never grows old.

AT THE GATE.

SOMETIMES, when the warm, toilsome day is done,
  We linger long beneath the twilight sky;
The air is chill, for vanished is the sun,
  Our limbs are weary and our home is nigh,
Our smiling home, where loved ones watch and wait,
  Yet, stand we, not unhappy, at the gate.

And thus our friend revered, whose task is o'er,
  The burden of a century's joy and pain,
We see, still pausing by the open door,
  To look on earth's familiar scenes again;
Fair is the home beyond, where loved ones wait,
  Yet rest the little hands upon the gate.

The twilight deepens; night comes on apace.
  We cross, with hasting steps, the threshold o'er
A joyous welcome beams from every face
  And we remember care and toil no more;
In the sweet atmosphere of peace we bide
  And all our earthly need is satisfied.

This patient friend, who waits the Master's will,
   Bearing the sheaves of many a weary year,
We would detain a little longer still
   · Till the completed century appear ;
But, if earth's skies grow dark, Heaven will be bright,
   And welcome her to all its love and light.

CONTENTS.